# Table of Contents

# INTRODUCTION

Across various West African countries, when there's heavily scent in the air with the delicious aroma of a flavourful rice. This can mean only one thing – jollof rice. Jollof rice is almost everyone's favourite dish in some countries in the region. No wonder there's always jollof rice war going on between Ghana and Nigeria, sometimes, Senegal, too. From street food vendors to high-end restaurants, jollof rice is an important aspect of Nigerian life and one of the most recognisable Nigerian exports. Known as ceebu jen in Senegal, jollof across West Africa have their own traditional twists and often local ingredients to make the jollof rice recipes personalized to a particular country. But all, mostly contain a combination of thyme, curry powder, scotch bonnet and bouillon cubes. Beef, chicken, pork or fish can be used in cooking jollof rice, some even do the assorted meat.

There's hardly any ceremony without the presence of jollof rice, unless you're trying too hard to make enemies. Like the saying goes – in the end you cannot make everyone happy, you're not jollof rice. An African food so popular that it has become the continent's greatest culinary export.

This book contains series of ways to cook sumptuous Jollof rice.

# CHAPTER ONE

## ORIGIN AND HISTORY

Africa's food scene is a wide and varied edible landscape, and the biggest treat awaits the foodies. Jollof rice is a common African food consumed throughout the West African region. You will always see it in parties, weddings, birthdays, etc. Jollof rice is called riz au gras in some of the French West Africa areas. However, it is called ceebu jen in Senegal and Gambia. The name Jollof is said to be driven from the Wolof people, a name that trace back to Jolof Empire of the Senegambian region. Over the years other cultures have added their influence to this regional dish, and it continue to thrive today as a landmark recipe within African cuisine.

The origins of jollof rice can be traced to the Senegambian region that was ruled by the Wolof or Jolof Empire in the 14th century, spanning parts of today's Senegal, The Gambia and Mauritania, where rice was grown. The dish has its roots in a traditional dish called thieboudienne, containing rice, fish, shellfish and vegetables.

Food and agriculture historian James C. McCann considers this claim plausible given the popularity of rice in the upper Niger valley, but considers it unlikely that the dish could have spread from Senegal to its current range since such a diffusion is not seen in "linguistic, historical or political patterns".

Instead he proposes that the dish spread with the Mali empire, especially the Djula tradespeople who dispersed widely to the regional commercial and urban centers, taking with them economic arts of "blacksmithing, small-scale marketing, and rice agronomy" as well as the religion of Islam.

Marc Dufumier, Emeritus Professor of Agronomy proposes a more recent origin for the dish, which may only have appeared as a consequence of the colonial promotion of intensive peanut cropping in central Senegal for the French oil industry, and where commensurate reduction in the planted area of traditional millet and sorghum staples was compensated by forced imports of broken rice from Southeast Asia.

It may then have spread throughout the region through the historical commercial, cultural and religious channels linking Senegal with Ghana, Nigeria and beyond, many of which continue to thrive today, such as the Tijāniyyah Sufi brotherhood bringing thousands of West African pilgrims to Senegal annually.

## GEOGRAPHICAL RANGE AND VARIANTS

Jollof rice is one of the most common dishes in West Africa. There are several regional variations in name and ingredients, for example, in Mali it is called zaamè in Bamanankan. The dish's most common name of Jollof derives from the name of the Wolof people, though in Senegal and Gambia the dish is referred to in Wolof as ceebu jën or benachin. In French-speaking areas, it is called riz au gras. Despite the variations, the dish is "mutually intelligible" across the regions and has become the best known African dish outside the continent.

Jollof rice traditionally consists of rice, cooking oil, vegetables such as tomato, onion, red pepper, garlic, ginger and scotch bonnet chilli peppers. To enhance the colour of the dish, tomato paste (purée) is added. As seasoning spices, salt, seasoning/stock cubes (a blend of flavour enhancers, salt, nutmeg and herbs), curry powder and dried thyme are used. To complement the dish, chicken, turkey, beef or fish are often served with the dish.

## REGIONAL VARIATIONS AND RIVALRY

Each West African country has at least one variant form of the dish, with Ghana, Nigeria, Sierra Leone, Liberia and Cameroon particularly competitive as to which country makes the best jollof. This is especially prominent between Nigeria and Ghana, in a rivalry dubbed the "Jollof Wars".

### Nigerian jollof

Although considerable variation exists, the basic profile for Nigerian jollof rice includes long grain parboiled rice, tomatoes and tomato paste, pepper, vegetable oil, onions, and stock cubes. Most of the ingredients are cooked in one pot, of which a rich meat stock and a fried tomato and pepper puree characteristically forms the base. Rice is then added and left to cook in the liquid. The dish is then served with the protein of choice and very often with fried plantains, moi moi, steamed vegetables, coleslaw, salad, etc. In the riverine areas of Nigeria where seafood is the main source of protein, seafood often takes the place of chicken or meat as the protein of choice.

## Ghanaian jollof

Ghanaian jollof rice is made of vegetable oil, onion, bell pepper, cloves of pressed garlic, chillies, tomato paste, beef or goat meat or chicken (some times alternated with mixed vegetables), local or refined rice and black pepper. The method of cooking jollof begins with first preparing the beef or chicken by seasoning and frying it until it is well-cooked. The rest of the ingredients are then fried all together, starting from onions, pepper, tomato paste, tomatoes and spices in that order. After all the ingredients have been fried, rice is then added and cooked until the meal is prepared. Ghanaian jollof is typically served with side dishes of beef, chicken, well-seasoned fried fish, or mixed vegetables.

Jollof in Ghana is also served alongside shito, a popular type of pepper which originates from Ghana, and salad during parties and other ceremonies.

## Rice's Effects on Weight Loss Are Conflicting

While brown rice's effects on weight loss are pretty well established, white rice's effects are not. People who eat whole grains like brown rice have repeatedly been shown to weigh less than those who don't, as well as be at a reduced risk of weight gain.

This could be attributed to the fiber, nutrients and plant compounds found in whole grains. They may increase feelings of fullness and help you eat fewer calories at a time. One 12-year study in women observed that those with the highest intake of dietary fiber from whole-grain foods had almost a 50% lower risk of major weight gain, compared to those with the lowest intake.

It has also been suggested that eating brown rice instead of white may lead to weight loss and more favorable blood fat levels. However, when it comes to white rice, the studies are a little more inconsistent. Numerous studies have shown that a dietary pattern high in refined grains like white rice is linked to weight gain and obesity. At the same time, other studies have not found a link between white rice or refined grain consumption and weight gain or central obesity. In fact, white rice consumption has even been linked to a reduced risk of weight gain, especially in countries where it's a staple food.

One study in overweight Korean women showed that a weight loss diet that included either white rice or mixed rice (brown and black) three times per day resulted in weight loss. The mixed-rice group lost 14.8 pounds (6.7 kg) over a six-week period, while the white-rice group lost 11.9 pounds (5.4 kg). Therefore, it appears that both types can be included in a weight loss diet. Nevertheless, brown rice has the advantage of being higher in fiber and nutrients than white rice, making it the healthier choice. Brown rice has been linked to weight loss and favorable blood fat levels. Most studies have found either no link between white rice and weight change or associated it with weight loss.

### Rice Was the Cornerstone of One Popular Weight Loss Diet

Interestingly, there was once a popular weight loss diet centered on white rice. Developed in 1939 to treat patients with high blood pressure and kidney disease, this ultra low-fat diet was called the Rice Diet. It was a tasteless, low-calorie diet that consisted mainly of white rice, fruit, fruit juice and sugar. Nonetheless, it had surprising effects on health, including weight loss and the relief of kidney disease symptoms. However, it should be noted that this was a very restrictive, low-fat, low-calorie diet. Therefore, the results may not be applicable to eating rice as part of a regular diet.

Nevertheless, it goes to show that rice can fit well into a weight loss diet if calorie intake is controlled. The Rice Diet was a popular and restrictive low-calorie diet that was used to relieve high blood pressure and symptoms of kidney disease.

## Rice Is a Staple Food in Many Countries

Rice is a staple food for more than half of the world's population, particularly Asian countries like China, Japan, Korea and India. These are all countries that, until recently, had relatively low percentages of people who were overweight or obese. White rice is the predominant source of carbs in those countries. For example, Koreans consume almost 40% of their total calorie intake from rice. In these countries, rice may be consumed an average of 20 times per week and up to six times per day.

Even so, rice consumption seems to protect against weight gain and high blood pressure in these populations. In elderly Chinese people, a dietary pattern high in rice and vegetables seems to help prevent weight gain, large waist circumference and obesity. The same results were found in a study including over 200 overweight Iranians. No association between the frequency of white rice consumption and body mass index or belly fat was found.

However, this trend may be changing, as diets in these countries become influenced by the Western Diet. In fact, the numbers of overweight and obese people have skyrocketed in many of these countries in the past few years. One study among Iranian adolescents showed that those who had the highest rice intake had the worst diet quality. This indicates that these adolescents may be consuming rice with foods that older generations did not eat, potentially leading to weight gain. At this point, it seems that rice intake itself has a neutral effect, while its health effects — positive or negative — depend on a person's overall diet. In short, it can be fattening if eaten with an unhealthy diet, but weight loss friendly if eaten with a healthy and well-balanced diet.

In Asian countries, rice is consumed up to six times per day. Rice consumption seems to protect against weight gain in these populations.

## Some Types May Spike Blood Sugar Levels

The glycemic index (GI) is a measure of how much and how quickly a food spikes your blood sugar levels. Foods high on the glycemic index cause rapid spikes in blood sugar levels and have been linked to overeating and weight gain.

On the other hand, foods with a low glycemic index cause a more gradual increase in blood sugar levels. They are believed to be particularly beneficial for people with diabetes, as they control blood sugar and insulin levels.

Generally speaking, whole grains have lower GI scores than refined grains. This is one of the reasons why diets high in whole grains have been linked to a 20–30% reduced risk of developing type 2 diabetes. That being said, not all studies have found a link between refined grain consumption and risk factors for type 2 diabetes.

The starch composition of rice may be a key factor in explaining this. Sticky rice is generally high in the starch amylopectin, which has a high GI. Therefore, it's rapidly digested and may cause blood sugar spikes.

Alternatively, non-sticky rice is high in amylose and has a low GI, which slows down the digestion of starch. It may even contain resistant starch, which is a type of healthy fiber. So regardless of whether rice is white or brown, its GI can range from relatively low to very high, depending on the type and variety.

Interestingly, one study in the UK that measured the GI response to 11 different types of rice found that white basmati rice was a low-GI food, while other brown and white varieties were classified as medium or high on the GI. If you are diabetic or sensitive to blood sugar spikes, picking non-sticky rice, which is high in amylose, would be your best bet to keep your blood sugar levels in check. Rice can rank either relatively low or high on the glycemic index scale. Non-sticky rices have lower GI levels than sticky rices do.

There is nothing particularly "fattening" about rice, so its effects on weight must come down to serving size and the overall quality of your diet. Studies have repeatedly shown that serving food in a larger container or dish increases intake, regardless of the food or drink being served. This has to do with the perception of the serving size. Serving large portions has been shown to increase calorie intake significantly, without people realizing it. Also, since people don't realize that they are eating more than usual, they generally don't compensate by eating less at the next meal. One interesting study showed that participants who didn't know they were eating soup from a self-refilling bowl ate 73% more soup than those eating from normal bowls. Most importantly, they didn't realize that they ate more than the others or perceive themselves as more full than those eating from normal bowls.

Studies that have analyzed the effects of serving size have shown that reducing the size of the "rice bowl" is an effective way to reduce calorie intake, body weight and blood sugar levels.

Therefore, depending on the serving size, rice can be both weight loss friendly and fattening

## HOW TO COOK JOLLOF RICE THE GHANAIAN WAY
**METHODS**

1 Ghanaian Jollof Rice

2 Preparing the meat

3 Creating the stew

Jollof (jol-ôf) rice is a popular dish that is enjoyed by Ghanaians, Nigerians, and other West Africans. Ghana is one of the several coastal countries of West Africa. Jollof has many variations; the dish can be made with meat, vegetables, or tofu. The uniquely colored rice is often enjoyed at dinnertime, but is also eaten at various parties and weddings. The origins of this dish stem from the Wolof people, an ethnic group found in the Senegambian region (Senegal and Gambia). Although most people know this dish as jollof, another name is benachin, which means "one pot" in the Wolof language. No matter the name, people from all over West Africa and -- now by emigration -- the world revel in this dish, whether it be at parties or in the comfort of their own homes.

**Ingredients**

Ghanaian jollof rice

Cooking oil

Onion

Chili pepper

Green pepper (bell pepper/capsicum pepper)

Fresh/ canned chopped tomatoes

Tomato puree

Stock cube

Salt

Water

Any other spice of your choice

Any other vegetable of your choice

Rice

Meat Preparation:

1 ½ jumbo onion, diced

1 habanero pepper, de-stemmed

3 lbs smoked turkey

7 cups water

¾ tablespoon salt

Creating the Stew:

2 cans Hunt's tomato sauce

½ jumbo onion, diced

1 habanero pepper, diced and de-stemmed

¼ cup of oil

¾ tablespoon salt

Meat broth (from meat preparation step):

½ clove garlic

Adding the rice:


6 cups jasmine rice

½ clove garlic

2 cups water

¼ tablespoon salt

Method

Blend chili pepper and fresh/canned chopped tomatoes. Chop the onion, green pepper and any other vegetables into small pieces.

Pour the cooking oil of your choice in a saucepan and heat it. Add the chopped onions and green pepper pieces. Leave on the fire till you start smelling the green pepper.

Pour in the blended chili pepper and allow to simmer till it just begins to fry. Pour in the blended fresh/canned chopped tomatoes. Add the tomato puree. Allow to simmer.

When the stew thickens, add the stock cube and any other spice. Taste before adding salt to know if the salt already added is sufficient. Keep stirring to ensure that the stew does not burn.

Pour in the rice and stir, ensuring the rice has properly mixed with the stew. Keep stirring till you feel the rice has soaked up the flavours of the stew.

Add enough water to cook the rice. Taste to check the salt content again and cover the saucepan. Allow to boil.

Keep checking the progress to ensure that the rice cooks properly. Once the water drains from the rice and its softness or hardness pleases you, it is ready to be served.

**Preparing the meat**

Add 1 diced jumbo onion, 1 habanero pepper, 3 lbs smoked turkey, and ¾ tablespoons salt to a large pot.

Add 7 cups water, or just enough water to cover the top of the meat in the pot.

Cover and simmer for 45 to 60 minutes on medium-high heat. Or, cook until the broth in the pot is an inch (2.5cm) from the bottom. Be sure to watch the broth level! Make sure that the broth does not fall too low.

Turn off the stove. Set aside the meat and broth.

**Creating the stew**

Add ¼ cup oil to another pot. Turn the heat on medium-high.

When the oil gets hot, add ½ diced jumbo onion.

Spoon onions onto the cooked turkey.

Sauté the onions and turkey for 4 to 5 minutes, or until golden brown.

Let simmer for 1 hour on medium heat. Stir every 10 to 15 minutes.

After simmering for 1 hour, add the broth (from the meat preparation section), ¾ tablespoon salt, and ½ clove of garlic to the pot.

Stir and let simmer for 1 more hour. Stir every 10 minutes.

Watch the stew level. If the stew level gets below the halfway mark of the pot, add the water and salt as needed, to keep the levels high enough.

**Adding the Rice**

Add 6 cups jasmine rice to a bowl and wash the rice. Add the rice to the stew by the spoonful, then add a quarter tablespoon of salt.

Be sure that enough rice is added. Also, do not add too much rice, or the dish will not cook well.

The rice level should stay 1- 1 ½ inches below the stew level, to avoid dryness.

Cover and let cook for 20 minutes on low heat. If, after 20 minutes, the rice is still hard or grainy, then mix a ½ a teaspoon of salt and 1 cup of water together and sprinkle over the rice.

Cook for 15 more minutes on low heat. Keep adding water on rice until rice is soft.

Check the texture. The rice should now have a characteristic orange color. Add the ½ a clove of garlic to the rice. Let it cook for 10 more minutes.

How To Prepare Salad For Jollof Rice?
How do you prepare salad? Instructions

The greens should be completely dry.

The greens should be bite-sized.

Put the greens in a really big bowl.

Add any other vegetables you like (make sure they are dry too).

Always dress your salad.

Most dressings need a touch of sweetness.

Taste the dressing first.

How do you make Jollof rice not sticky? If you are ever in a sticky situation, here are some tips: 1. Too Much Water But Good Texture: If there is too much water in your Jollof, but the texture is just right. Transfer the rice to a wider pot (if possible), increase the heat to maximum and leave UNCOVERED.

What is jollof rice served with? Ghanaian jollof is typically served with side dishes of beef, chicken, well-seasoned fried fish, or mixed vegetables. Jollof in Ghana is also served alongside shito, a popular type of pepper which originates from Ghana, and salad during parties and other ceremonies.

## How do you parboil rice for jollof rice?

This is the method to follow to parboil rice meant for preparing jollof rice recipes:

Wash the rice in cold water (optional) and place in a pot.

Add some water, about 4 times the level of the rice.

Set on the stove and leave to cook.

Note when the water starts boiling and leave to cook till the rice is rubbery.

## What are the 4 types of salads?

Four types are generally sold: Iceberg, Butterhead, Romaine, and Leaf. Iceberg – lettuce is by far the major type.

## What is the best time to eat salad?

Eating a salad before your meal may help with weight loss

### What do I do if my jollof rice is soggy?

If you're afraid that it is really soggy, then place it in a cool place such as an open fridge (closing the fridge means that condensation will pull on your food, so don't). You might want to throw the cooled down rice in the oven so that it completely dries out for good measure.

### What does jollof rice taste like?

This dish is legendary for its smoky taste. This dish is cooked over a fire wood and allowed to burn at the bottom to give it a smoky flavour. A significant spice used in cooking the Nigerian Jollof is the bay leaf, which also adds to its rich smoky flavour.

### What country has the best jollof rice?

The main protagonists in a steam over who makes the best Jollof rice are Ghana, Nigeria, Sierra Leone, Liberia and Cameroon. The Gambia and Senegal are quite laid-back and rarely enter the Jollof controversy; after all, they gave it to the world.

### What country made jollof rice first?

Senegal's

Jollof's origins can be traced to Senegal's ancient Wolof empire and medieval state in the 1300s, where it first surfaced as a dish called thiéboudienne. As the Wolof empire grew and dispersed along the West African coast and region, so did the recipe, which was named after one of the biggest Wolof states, Jolof.

### How long does it take for rice to parboil?

Once the water is boiling, cook for about 4-6 minutes or until the tips of a rice grain is clear. Pour the parboiled rice out into a strainer and rinse with lukewarm water to rinse off some salt and to slow the cooking process.

### How many minutes should I parboil rice?

5 minutes

Bring a saucepan 3/4 of the way full of clean, cold water to a boil. Add a pinch of salt to the water. Add rice to the water and boil for 5 minutes. Drain and cool.

### Is it good to parboil rice before cooking?

Parboiling rice ensures that your rice does not burn before it is done; it prevents you getting burnt, soggy and undercooked rice. Parboiling rice also gets rid of the excess starch in the rice thereby eliminating the cardboard taste associated with rice that wasn't well washed before cooking.

What are 5 types of salads?
Types of salads

Green salad.

Fruit salads.

Rice and pasta salads.

Bound salads.

Dinner salads.

Dessert salads.

What are main course salad qualities?
Main Course Salad is characterized as: usually containing a portion of protein, such as chicken breast , slices of beef, force meats etc. Other specific high-protein foods that can be included in the Main Course salad: fish, eggs, legumes, and cheese.

Is it okay to eat salad everyday?
As long as you're incorporating a wide variety of ingredients (different types of veggies, fruits, beans, legumes, nuts and seeds, protein sources, etc.) and regularly switching things up, that daily salad can easily be a nutritional powerhouse

that supplies many of the vitamins and minerals your body needs.

### Can you lose belly fat by eating salad?

Eating salad does burn fat when you combine your salad with healthy grains for a full and complete meal. When you combine a portion of healthy vegetables with your meals–be it pasta or a sandwich– you will be surprised to see what an incredible difference this can make on your lean body transformation.

### Is it OK to have salad at night?

You can have a pre-bed food such salad filled with lettuce, berries, cottage cheese, and honey are delicious and extremely healthy. Besides, lettuce is filled with lactucarium which has sedative properties. It soothes the body and helps it to get relaxing sleep for the night.

### Health Benefits of Jollof Rice

When you Google "Health Benefits of Jollof Rice" (because you're feeling guilty about the copious amounts of Jollof Rice you're consuming), you get recipes. Recipes, I tell you. No one has bothered to write down the health benefits of Jollof Rice so I decided to do myself (and you) a favour by documenting them. This list is in no way, exhaustive. Feel free to add your own health benefits.

Jollof Rice makes you happy. A study carried out in my house showed that family members are generally happier when lunch (or dinner) is shown to be Jollof Rice. It may be related to the release of oxytocin in the brain as our eyes register the pleasure that is a steaming heap of sinfully orange rice. And fried plantain.

Jollof Rice contains tomatoes, peppers and onions. Tomatoes are good for you. They help prevent cancer. Peppers are good for you. They contain lots of vitamins. Onions are good for you. They reduce inflammation and heal infections.

Jollof Rice brings back good memories, very key to good mental health. Think about it. Do you have any bad memories associated with jollof rice? Now think about eba. Or beans. Ehen. Jollof Rice goes well with red wine, which is good for your heart. Jollof Rice (when done properly) burns your pots. Scrubbing those pots is a workout for getting toned arms.

Jollof Rice is a confidence booster, if you were worried about your less than stellar cooking record. Almost anyone can cook it, you don't need to be a 5-star Michelin chef. It is very forgiving. It is almost impossible to mess up. I would have said impossible to mess up, but look at Jamie Oliver.

# CHAPTER TWO

## DIFFERENT JOLLOF RICE RECIPES

### How to make jollof rice at home

Jollof offers a real eclectic mix of West African cultures and people and its combined history has grown to become the best tasting food in the region. But you don't have wait until your next vacation in the region to eat some jollof rice, making an authentic jollof rice at home can be attempted by everyone, might not be easy as your everyday rice recipe. Yes, we know not everyone has the cooking skills to do that at home, but it is still perfectly possible to create good jollof rice at home. It is always far more rewarding to make your own, and much more fun. Up your jollof cooking game and add this delicious dish to your repertoire with Dream

Africa's handy prep guide to learn how to make the BEST jollof rice recipe.

Jollof rice recipe
Ingredients

for 4 servings

2 ½ cups long grain parboiled rice

½ cup vegetable oil

1.5kg beef. Alternatively you can use chicken pieces, or whole chicken

Diced tomato, 400g

Tomato paste, 150g

1 habanero pepper

2 teaspoons curry powder

2 teaspoons thyme

1 teaspoon garlic powder

1 teaspoon ground ginger

2 Maggi/Knorr cubes

Pepper to taste

Salt to taste

Preparation

Wash the meat, then wash and cut it into desired chunks.

Cook meat with the thyme, seasoning cubes, onions and all other ingredients for the meat seasoning. Cook until meat is well done. Separate meat from the stock.

Wash your rice in hot water and rinse with cold water. Parboil just to have it semi-cooked. Rinse the parboiled rice and put in a sieve to drain.

Slice the tomatoes, paprika and peppers – then blend it all together. Pour the mixture in a pot and cook till it thickens. This is to reduce excess water in the blended mixture.

Heat up some oil in a new pot, add and stir-fry the sliced onions and basil leaves.

Add rosemary, bay leaves, seasoning cube, then stir-in tomato mixture. Cook till everything is well fried and giving the stew flavour.

Add the meat stock, and some salt to taste. Add whatever ingredient and seasoning you think isn't sufficient, and adjust to taste.

Add the semi-cooked rice, spread it gently with a spoon. Add some more water for steaming, if necessary. You might be adding extra water as the rice cooks so do not add so much.

Add the meat stir well to incorporate, and cook together with the rice, this allows all the flavour to blend together and makes meat extra tender.

Allow to cook on a medium heat. Jollof rice tends to burn quickly, to avoid this don't stir until it has cooked through.

Cover the pot and leave to cook on low to medium heat. This way the rice does not burn before the water dries up.

Serve jollof rice with fried meat, boiled eggs, dodo (fried plantain), if desired.

Enjoy


Ingredient

1 tablespoon olive oil

1 large onion, sliced

2 (14.5 ounce) cans stewed tomatoes

½ (6 ounce) can tomato paste

1 teaspoon salt

¼ teaspoon black pepper

¼ teaspoon cayenne pepper

½ teaspoon red pepper flakes

1 tablespoon Worcestershire sauce

1 teaspoon chopped fresh rosemary

2 cups water

1 (3 pound) whole chicken, cut into 8 pieces

1 cup uncooked white rice

1 cup diced carrots

½ pound fresh green beans, trimmed and snapped into 1 to 2 inch pieces

¼ teaspoon ground nutmeg

Directions

## Step 1

Pour oil into large saucepan. Cook onion in oil over medium-low heat until translucent.

## Step 2

Stir in stewed tomatoes and tomato paste, and season with salt, black pepper, cayenne pepper, red pepper flakes, Worcestershire sauce and rosemary. Cover, and bring to a boil. Reduce heat, stir in water, and add chicken pieces. Simmer for 30 minutes.

## Step 3

Stir in rice, carrots, and green beans, and season with nutmeg. Bring to a boil, then reduce heat to low. Cover, and simmer until the chicken is fork-tender and the rice is cooked, 25 to 30 minutes

Jollof Rice

Ingredients

1 pound parboiled rice

1 can tomato puree-400 grams

1 onion, sliced

3 cloves garlic

4 teaspoons olive oil

6 small or 3 large red bell peppers, seeded and sliced

1 bunch thyme, leaves picked

1 teaspoon white pepper

8 chicken bouillon cubes (recommended: Maggi or Goya)

Directions

With blender, blend tomatoes, onions, red pepper, and garlic until smooth. Add bouillon cubes, thyme and white pepper.

Add olive oil to the blended paste, and set the mixture aside. Add 4 cups of water into a pot.

Wash the rice in hot water until the water is clear. Drain through a fine sieve.

Pour the rice and blended mixture into the pot of water and stir with wooden spoon. Set the stove to medium heat and place pot on stove, then let it cook for 45 minutes while stirring every 15 minutes.

Ingredients

for 6 servings

2 large yellow onions, roughly chopped

⅓ cup vegetable oil (80 mL), plus 2 tablespoons, divided

14 oz diced tomato (395 g), 2 cans

6 oz tomato paste (170 g), 1 can

1 habanero pepper

2 teaspoons curry powder

1 teaspoon garlic powder

1 teaspoon ground ginger

½ teaspoon mixed dried herbs

3 chicken bouillon cubes, crushed

2 ½ cups long grain rice (500 g), rinsed

1 cup frozen mixed vegetable (150 g)

1 ½ cups water (360 mL)

Preparation

Add onions and 2 tablespoons of oil to a blender and pulse until smooth. Transfer to a medium bowl.

Add the diced tomatoes, tomato paste, and habanero pepper to the blender, and pulse until smooth. Transfer to a separate medium bowl.

Heat the remaining ⅓ cup (80 ml) of oil in a large, heavy-bottomed pot over medium heat.

Once the oil is shimmering, add the onion puree and cook until the water has cooked out and the puree is starting to brown, about 10 minutes.

Stir in the tomato puree and add the curry powder, garlic powder, ginger, dried herbs, and crushed bouillon cubes. Cook for 20-30 minutes, stirring occasionally, until the stew has reduced by half and is deep red in color.

Add the rice, mixed vegetables, and water. Bring to a boil, then reduce the heat to low and cover the pot with foil and a lid. Simmer for another 30 minutes, until the rice is cooked through and the liquid is absorbed.

Enjoy!

## CONCLUSION

There doesn't seem to be anything specifically fattening about rice. Different studies link it to both weight loss and weight gain. However, of the two types of rice, there is no question that brown rice is much more nutritious than white rice.

Non-sticky rice may also be the better choice for people who are sensitive to blood sugar swings or have diabetes. It all seems to boil down to watching your serving size and following an overall healthy and balanced diet.

CPSIA information can be obtained
at www.ICGtesting.com
Printed in the USA
LVHW051752151121
703397LV00014B/462

9 798488 734517